Fulfilling the Dream

A Daily Journey Towards Success

Líderes
—del—
Futuro

Rafael Vázquez Guzmán

Thank you for choosing this journal. In life there will always be new challenges that we will face on a daily basis. Our attitude towards these events will have a great effect on whether or not we will be successful with them. While we cannot control all the factors, our childhood experiences can affect how we react to challenging situations.

The goal of this journal is for you to begin a journey of success. We all have regrets, traumas, successes and goals that guide our view of the world. Healing is a lifetime process that requires us to do daily work in order to reach happiness and fulfillment. We all have the right to be successful in our own way without judgement of others. For some individuals, success comes from living a long life to then be able to enjoy moments with great-grandchildren. For others, success may be achieved when they finally get to run their own business and have the final say in decision making. At the end, we all have different views on how success can be reached. But most importantly, we should know we are all capable of succeeding in this world. We must go through the journey of developing the right skills to accomplish our success.

This journal is not meant to replace formal therapy, but as one more tool that can facilitate the process of healing. I am not a therapist, but I have worked for 24 years with families and youth who have had challenges at school, with the criminal justice system and with their families. My work with these families has been to create healthy forms of communication as a stepping-stone for atonement. While this has not always been possible, I have never given up. Many of the youth I have worked with have never experienced love, affection, and respect and their outburst are a call for help. I've also worked for ten years with people in prisons who have shared the consequences that childhood trauma has left on them. I decided to create this journal for you to identify the positive parts of your life and the challenges you must overcome. Journaling has worked for many individuals as a form of meditation and has helped them to finally feel comfortable with putting their thoughts on paper. Seeing it on paper can be challenging, as it makes trauma and barriers more real, but it also provides an opportunity to finally work on some of the barriers that have kept you from fulfilling your dreams. Journaling also provides the opportunity to recognize the small successes, which is the best way to work towards one final goal.

I recognize part of this process will be painful and triggering, but I also know it can take you a step closer towards healing. If the work you begin here becomes overwhelming, always remember that the National Suicide Prevention Hotline is just a phone call away at (800) 273-8255.

For deaf or hard of hearing individuals, use your preferred relay system or dial 711. Also, if you find that this work is too challenging to do alone, please consider reaching out for therapy. Some of our traumas have been with us for years or decades and it will require the assistance of a professional to guide us through this work. The journal can be a great tool for you to use as you attend therapy.

Regrets

Many individuals live their lives with regret to their last dying breath. These regrets could include not taking on that employment opportunity that presented itself sometime in the past and that would have improved income and increased assets or provide for an early retirement. I have met many individuals who were given the opportunity to pursue higher education, but due to many factors, did not pursue this opportunity. Years later, some of them have come back to try college because they are now clear about their needs and their goals. Finally, I have also met many individuals who did not have confidence in themselves and therefore never pursued friendships with individuals who would have increased their level of happiness and pushed them to reach their goals.

We all have some regrets. Some of them are more serious than others, but we can either learn to let go of them or forgive ourselves for these regrets. Not letting go will only allow us to keep blaming ourselves and may never be able to outgrow those mistakes. I have met individuals who came back to school to obtain their GED (High School Diploma Equivalent) in their mid-sixties and then go on to obtain college diplomas. They noticed they were not happy and did not want to continue to limit themselves the rest of their lives. I am glad that they were able and willing to do this because it gave them the opportunity to be role models for family members and friends.

Negative Behaviors

Many of us who experienced trauma in childhood were never given the opportunity to heal and therefore learned to cope with it in unhealthy ways. Coping is not healing, but a way to get through a stressful experience and for some individuals, to get through the day. Among the most common coping mechanisms are drinking alcohol, smoking cigarettes, consuming marijuana, playing videogames, and watching television as ways to escape from reality. Watching television once in a while is different from sitting daily for several hours and being entertained. This time could have been used to read or have a side business that could lead to financial independence. It is not to blame anyone for this behavior, but to understand that unhealthy behavior does not lead to a positive outcome. The sooner we understand this, the faster we will be able to start our healing process.

People in Our Lives

Part of beginning the process of healing and planning for the future requires us to sit down and conduct an assessment of individuals in our lives who contribute to a positive lifestyle. This also means realizing who the individuals are who may have a different life-long interests than us, which can mean taking a step back from them. Some of them may be family members, friends, acquaintances, or coworkers. Due to many factors, we may not always be able to physically distance ourselves from them, but becoming aware of their influence and learning to create healthy boundaries can be helpful. Part of healing is learning to create plans A and B, which can relate to moving out of the house and moving in with healthy friends who can contribute to a positive lifestyle. It can also relate to changing employment because the environment may be detrimental to our mental and physical health. Many of us have been brought up to believe that to move out of the household is to turn your back on your family, but we must take care of ourselves before we are able to take care of our future children or aging parents. It is not selfish to take care of ourselves, but it is necessary to heal in order to support others towards success.

Successes

Not everything is negative and we must take the time to celebrate our successes. Waking up and making it to school or work is a success. Taking a walk or run is a form of success. I invite you to take your time to make a list of the successes you're proud of and work on how you can improve on them.

Sometimes we underestimate ourselves and our successes. The fact that you are reading this introduction and guidelines is a success. Graduating from school, obtaining a new career, buying a home, and being financially stable are all examples of successes. Take a moment and congratulate yourself for your many successes you are proud of and work on because the next step is planning for the future.

Goals

The last step of the healing process and preparing for the future is all based on goals. In the next few pages you will see a quick sample of a ten-year plan, but your goals may be many and can include additional education, starting a business, traveling, having a family and/or retirement. Each one is on a different path and the road may be long or short depending on your age at the moment of beginning this journey. There is nothing wrong with dreaming big even when you may be older. Advances in medicine have allowed us to live much longer and therefore, you cannot limit yourself.

I hope this journal will be the beginning of a long and enjoyable process towards success. Don't try to move too fast and remember that anything worth having takes time, patience and hard work.

The journal includes four parts for each day.

1. List one challenge that you faced today

2. List two items that went well today

3. List three things that you are grateful for today

4. Open space to write freely

In the next page you will find what I call the 10-Year plan. You can have many goals. Sit down and spend some time working on goals for the next month, six months, one year, three years, five years, seven years, and finally ten years. You may have multiple goals in your list and at first, it may be a challenge to complete the first month's goals, but it's about creating a routine and the discipline necessary to make it work. Do not allow yourself to become overwhelmed because you cannot think of all of your life goals. Write some of the ones that come to mind immediately and are realistic and then, comeback from time to time to add some more.

Finally, from time to time, there will be opportunities to do some more evaluations of your goals. Remember that this is not a solo journey, but the journal is meant to support you in reaching your goals. Identify individuals who will support you and who will validate your struggles and your successes.

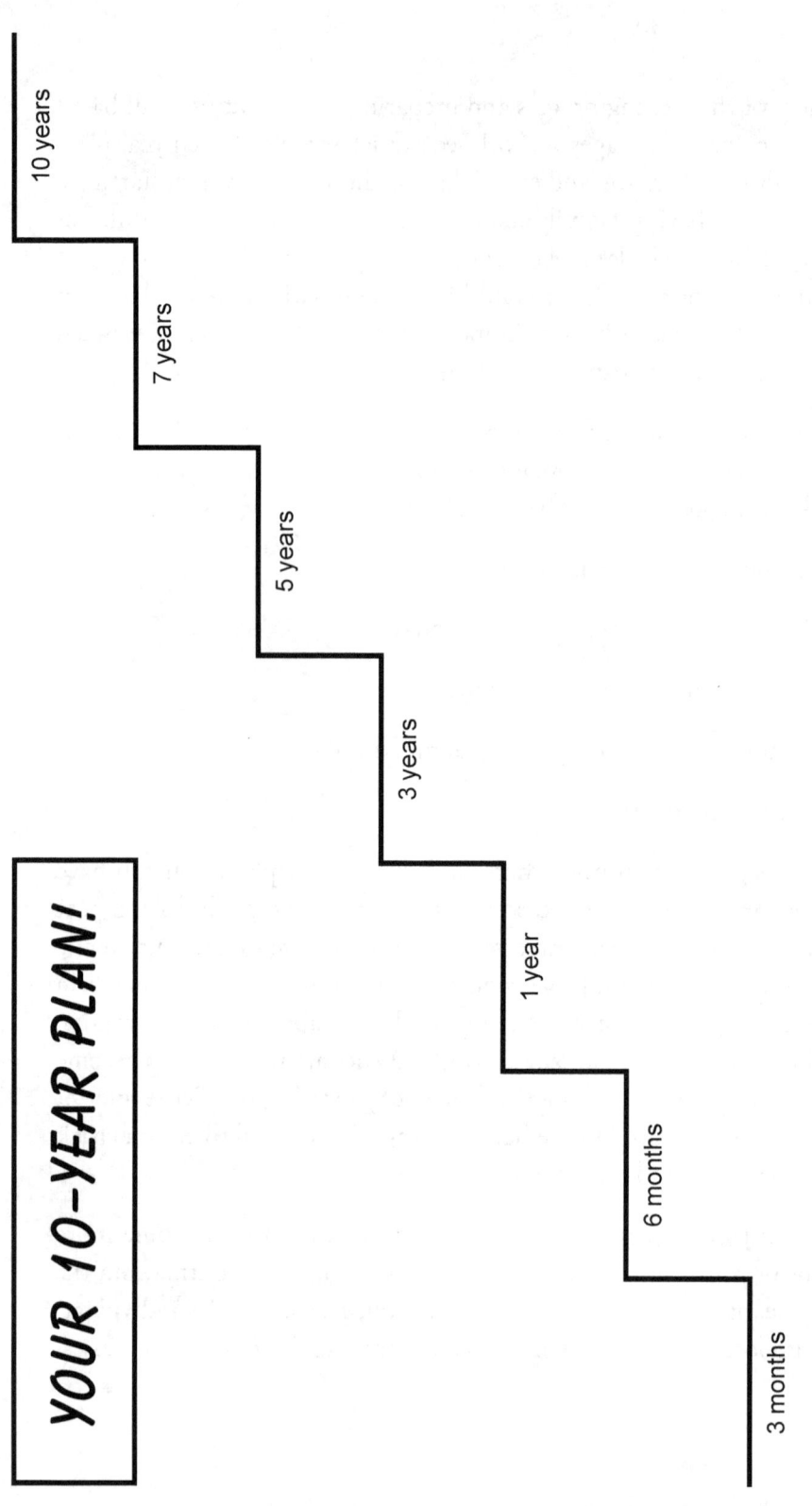

Today's Date: _____

List one challenge that you faced today

_____

List two items that went well today

_____

_____

List three things you are grateful for today

_____

_____

_____

Feel free to write any additional thoughts in this space

Today's Date: _____

List one challenge that you faced today
_____

List two items that went well today
_____
_____

List three things you are grateful for today
_____
_____
_____

Feel free to write any additional thoughts in this space

Today's Date: _____

List one challenge that you faced today

_____

List two items that went well today

_____

_____

List three things you are grateful for today

_____

_____

_____

Feel free to write any additional thoughts in this space

Today's Date: _____

List one challenge that you faced today
_____

List two items that went well today
_____

_____

List three things you are grateful for today
_____

_____

_____

Feel free to write any additional thoughts in this space

Today's Date: _____

List one challenge that you faced today
_____

List two items that went well today
_____
_____

List three things you are grateful for today
_____
_____
_____

Feel free to write any additional thoughts in this space

Today's Date: _____

List one challenge that you faced today

_____

List two items that went well today

_____

_____

List three things you are grateful for today

_____

_____

_____

Feel free to write any additional thoughts in this space

Today's Date: _____

You are on day 7 of this journey. You should feel great about sticking with the process. You will have an additional page to draw something for yourself. Art is not something that should be judge in a journal. It is for you and you only. Draw whatever you feel like drawing.

List one challenge that you faced today

_____

List two items that went well today

_____

_____

List three things you are grateful for today

_____

_____

_____

Feel free to write any additional thoughts in this space

(Remember, this is your space. Be creative.)

Today's Date: _____

List one challenge that you faced today
_____

List two items that went well today
_____
_____

List three things you are grateful for today
_____
_____
_____

Feel free to write any additional thoughts in this space

Today's Date: _____

List one challenge that you faced today

_____

List two items that went well today

_____

_____

List three things you are grateful for today

_____

_____

_____

Feel free to write any additional thoughts in this space

Today's Date: _____

List one challenge that you faced today

_____

List two items that went well today

_____

_____

List three things you are grateful for today

_____

_____

_____

Feel free to write any additional thoughts in this space

Today's Date: _____

List one challenge that you faced today
_____

List two items that went well today
_____

_____

List three things you are grateful for today
_____

_____

_____

Feel free to write any additional thoughts in this space

Today's Date: _____

List one challenge that you faced today
_____

List two items that went well today
_____
_____

List three things you are grateful for today
_____
_____
_____

Feel free to write any additional thoughts in this space

Today's Date: _____

List one challenge that you faced today

_____

List two items that went well today

_____

_____

List three things you are grateful for today

_____

_____

_____

Feel free to write any additional thoughts in this space

Today's Date: _____

List one challenge that you faced today
_____

List two items that went well today
_____
_____

List three things you are grateful for today
_____
_____
_____

Feel free to write any additional thoughts in this space

Today's Date: _____

List one challenge that you faced today

_____

List two items that went well today

_____

_____

List three things you are grateful for today

_____

_____

_____

Feel free to write any additional thoughts in this space

Today's Date: _____

List one challenge that you faced today

_____

List two items that went well today

_____

_____

List three things you are grateful for today

_____

_____

_____

Feel free to write any additional thoughts in this space

Today's Date: _____

List one challenge that you faced today
_____

List two items that went well today
_____

_____

List three things you are grateful for today
_____

_____

_____

Feel free to write any additional thoughts in this space

Today's Date: _____

List one challenge that you faced today

_____

List two items that went well today

_____

_____

List three things you are grateful for today

_____

_____

_____

Feel free to write any additional thoughts in this space

Today's Date: _____

List one challenge that you faced today

_____

List two items that went well today

_____

_____

List three things you are grateful for today

_____

_____

_____

Feel free to write any additional thoughts in this space

Today's Date: _____

List one challenge that you faced today

_____

List two items that went well today

_____

_____

List three things you are grateful for today

_____

_____

_____

Feel free to write any additional thoughts in this space

Today's Date: _____

List one challenge that you faced today
_____

List two items that went well today
_____

_____

List three things you are grateful for today
_____

_____

_____

Feel free to write any additional thoughts in this space

Today's Date: _____

List one challenge that you faced today

_____

List two items that went well today

_____

_____

List three things you are grateful for today

_____

_____

_____

Feel free to write any additional thoughts in this space

Today's Date: _____

List one challenge that you faced today
_____

List two items that went well today
_____

_____

List three things you are grateful for today
_____

_____

_____

Feel free to write any additional thoughts in this space

Today's Date: _____

List one challenge that you faced today
_____

List two items that went well today
_____

_____

List three things you are grateful for today
_____

_____

_____

Feel free to write any additional thoughts in this space

Today's Date: _____

List one challenge that you faced today
_____

List two items that went well today
_____
_____

List three things you are grateful for today
_____
_____
_____

Feel free to write any additional thoughts in this space

Today's Date: _____

List one challenge that you faced today

_____

List two items that went well today

_____

_____

List three things you are grateful for today

_____

_____

_____

Feel free to write any additional thoughts in this space

Today's Date: _____

List one challenge that you faced today

_____

List two items that went well today

_____

_____

List three things you are grateful for today

_____

_____

_____

Feel free to write any additional thoughts in this space

Today's Date: _____

List one challenge that you faced today
_____

List two items that went well today
_____

_____

List three things you are grateful for today
_____

_____

_____

Feel free to write any additional thoughts in this space

Today's Date: _____

List one challenge that you faced today
_____

List two items that went well today
_____
_____

List three things you are grateful for today
_____
_____
_____

Feel free to write any additional thoughts in this space

Today's Date: _____

You are on day 30 of your journaling. Have you completed the goal you set up for the first month? If so, take a moment to celebrate your success, as this is a great accomplishment. If not, then, come up with a list of ways you can do that will help you accomplish this goal in the next thirty days.

List one challenge that you faced today
_____

List two items that went well today
_____
_____

List three things you are grateful for today
_____
_____
_____

Feel free to write any additional thoughts in this space

Today's Date: _____

List one challenge that you faced today
_____

List two items that went well today
_____
_____

List three things you are grateful for today
_____
_____
_____

Feel free to write any additional thoughts in this space

Today's Date: _____

List one challenge that you faced today
_____

List two items that went well today
_____
_____

List three things you are grateful for today
_____
_____
_____

Feel free to write any additional thoughts in this space

Today's Date: _____

List one challenge that you faced today
_____

List two items that went well today
_____
_____

List three things you are grateful for today
_____
_____
_____

Feel free to write any additional thoughts in this space

Today's Date: _____

List one challenge that you faced today
_____

List two items that went well today
_____

_____

List three things you are grateful for today
_____

_____

_____

Feel free to write any additional thoughts in this space

Today's Date: _____

List one challenge that you faced today
_____

List two items that went well today
_____

_____

List three things you are grateful for today
_____

_____

_____

Feel free to write any additional thoughts in this space

Today's Date: _____

List one challenge that you faced today
_____

List two items that went well today
_____
_____

List three things you are grateful for today
_____
_____
_____

Feel free to write any additional thoughts in this space

Today's Date: _____

List one challenge that you faced today

_____

List two items that went well today

_____

_____

List three things you are grateful for today

_____

_____

_____

Feel free to write any additional thoughts in this space

Today's Date: _____

List one challenge that you faced today

_____

List two items that went well today

_____

_____

List three things you are grateful for today

_____

_____

_____

Feel free to write any additional thoughts in this space

Today's Date: _____

List one challenge that you faced today

_____

List two items that went well today

_____

_____

List three things you are grateful for today

_____

_____

_____

Feel free to write any additional thoughts in this space

Today's Date: _____

List one challenge that you faced today
_____

List two items that went well today
_____
_____

List three things you are grateful for today
_____
_____
_____

Feel free to write any additional thoughts in this space

Today's Date: _____

List one challenge that you faced today
_____

List two items that went well today
_____
_____

List three things you are grateful for today
_____
_____
_____

Feel free to write any additional thoughts in this space

Today's Date: _____

List one challenge that you faced today
_____

List two items that went well today
_____
_____

List three things you are grateful for today
_____
_____
_____

Feel free to write any additional thoughts in this space

Today's Date: _____

List one challenge that you faced today
_____

List two items that went well today
_____
_____

List three things you are grateful for today
_____
_____
_____

Feel free to write any additional thoughts in this space

Today's Date: _____

List one challenge that you faced today

_____

List two items that went well today

_____

_____

List three things you are grateful for today

_____

_____

_____

Feel free to write any additional thoughts in this space

Today's Date: _____

List one challenge that you faced today

_____

List two items that went well today

_____

_____

List three things you are grateful for today

_____

_____

_____

Feel free to write any additional thoughts in this space

Today's Date: _____

List one challenge that you faced today
_____

List two items that went well today
_____
_____

List three things you are grateful for today
_____
_____
_____

Feel free to write any additional thoughts in this space

Today's Date: _____

List one challenge that you faced today
_____

List two items that went well today
_____
_____

List three things you are grateful for today
_____
_____
_____

Feel free to write any additional thoughts in this space

Today's Date: _____

List one challenge that you faced today
_____

List two items that went well today
_____
_____

List three things you are grateful for today
_____
_____
_____

Feel free to write any additional thoughts in this space

Today's Date: _____

List one challenge that you faced today
_____

List two items that went well today
_____
_____

List three things you are grateful for today
_____
_____
_____

Feel free to write any additional thoughts in this space

Today's Date: _____

List one challenge that you faced today
_____

List two items that went well today
_____
_____

List three things you are grateful for today
_____
_____
_____

Feel free to write any additional thoughts in this space

Today's Date: _____

List one challenge that you faced today
_____

List two items that went well today
_____

_____

List three things you are grateful for today
_____

_____

_____

Feel free to write any additional thoughts in this space

Today's Date: _____

List one challenge that you faced today
_____

List two items that went well today
_____

_____

List three things you are grateful for today
_____

_____

_____

Feel free to write any additional thoughts in this space

Today's Date: _____

List one challenge that you faced today

_____

List two items that went well today

_____

_____

List three things you are grateful for today

_____

_____

_____

Feel free to write any additional thoughts in this space

Today's Date: _____

List one challenge that you faced today
_____

List two items that went well today
_____
_____

List three things you are grateful for today
_____
_____
_____

Feel free to write any additional thoughts in this space

Today's Date: _____

List one challenge that you faced today

_____

List two items that went well today

_____

_____

List three things you are grateful for today

_____

_____

_____

Feel free to write any additional thoughts in this space

Today's Date: _____

List one challenge that you faced today
_____

List two items that went well today
_____
_____

List three things you are grateful for today
_____
_____
_____

Feel free to write any additional thoughts in this space

Today's Date: _____

List one challenge that you faced today

_____

List two items that went well today

_____

_____

List three things you are grateful for today

_____

_____

_____

Feel free to write any additional thoughts in this space

Today's Date: _____

List one challenge that you faced today

_____

List two items that went well today

_____

_____

List three things you are grateful for today

_____

_____

_____

Feel free to write any additional thoughts in this space

Today's Date: _____

List one challenge that you faced today
_____

List two items that went well today
_____
_____

List three things you are grateful for today
_____
_____
_____

Feel free to write any additional thoughts in this space

Today's Date: _____

You are on day 60 of your journey. Reflect on what you have accomplished and the things to be grateful for. Think of the new friendships you have made and about the bad habits you have left behind. Enjoy writing about this so you can comeback in a few months or even years and see your progression. I added an extra blank page for you to do something artistic.

List one challenge that you faced today
_____

List two items that went well today
_____
_____

List three things you are grateful for today
_____
_____
_____

Feel free to write any additional thoughts in this space

Today's Date: _____

List one challenge that you faced today
_____

List two items that went well today
_____

_____

List three things you are grateful for today
_____

_____

_____

Feel free to write any additional thoughts in this space

Today's Date: _____

List one challenge that you faced today
_____

List two items that went well today
_____

_____

List three things you are grateful for today
_____

_____

_____

Feel free to write any additional thoughts in this space

Today's Date: _____

List one challenge that you faced today
_____

List two items that went well today
_____

_____

List three things you are grateful for today
_____

_____

_____

Feel free to write any additional thoughts in this space

Today's Date: _____

List one challenge that you faced today
_____

List two items that went well today
_____
_____

List three things you are grateful for today
_____
_____
_____

Feel free to write any additional thoughts in this space

Today's Date: _____

List one challenge that you faced today
_____

List two items that went well today
_____

_____

List three things you are grateful for today
_____

_____

_____

Feel free to write any additional thoughts in this space

Today's Date: _____

List one challenge that you faced today
_____

List two items that went well today
_____
_____

List three things you are grateful for today
_____
_____
_____

Feel free to write any additional thoughts in this space

Today's Date: _____

List one challenge that you faced today
_____

List two items that went well today
_____

_____

List three things you are grateful for today
_____

_____

_____

Feel free to write any additional thoughts in this space

Today's Date: _____

List one challenge that you faced today
_____

List two items that went well today
_____
_____

List three things you are grateful for today
_____
_____
_____

Feel free to write any additional thoughts in this space

Today's Date: _____

List one challenge that you faced today

_____

List two items that went well today

_____

_____

List three things you are grateful for today

_____

_____

_____

Feel free to write any additional thoughts in this space

Today's Date: _____

List one challenge that you faced today
_____

List two items that went well today
_____

_____

List three things you are grateful for today
_____

_____

_____

Feel free to write any additional thoughts in this space

Today's Date: _____

List one challenge that you faced today

_____

List two items that went well today

_____

_____

List three things you are grateful for today

_____

_____

_____

Feel free to write any additional thoughts in this space

Today's Date: _____

List one challenge that you faced today

_____

List two items that went well today

_____

_____

List three things you are grateful for today

_____

_____

_____

Feel free to write any additional thoughts in this space

Today's Date: _____

List one challenge that you faced today
_____

List two items that went well today
_____
_____

List three things you are grateful for today
_____
_____
_____

Feel free to write any additional thoughts in this space

Today's Date: _____

List one challenge that you faced today
_____

List two items that went well today
_____

_____

List three things you are grateful for today
_____

_____

_____

Feel free to write any additional thoughts in this space

Today's Date: _____

List one challenge that you faced today
_____

List two items that went well today
_____

_____

List three things you are grateful for today
_____

_____

_____

Feel free to write any additional thoughts in this space

Today's Date: _____

List one challenge that you faced today
_____

List two items that went well today
_____

_____

List three things you are grateful for today
_____

_____

_____

Feel free to write any additional thoughts in this space

Today's Date: _____

List one challenge that you faced today
_____

List two items that went well today
_____

_____

List three things you are grateful for today
_____

_____

_____

Feel free to write any additional thoughts in this space

Today's Date: _____

List one challenge that you faced today
_____

List two items that went well today
_____
_____

List three things you are grateful for today
_____
_____
_____

Feel free to write any additional thoughts in this space

Today's Date: _____

List one challenge that you faced today

_____

List two items that went well today

_____

_____

List three things you are grateful for today

_____

_____

_____

Feel free to write any additional thoughts in this space

Today's Date: _____

List one challenge that you faced today

_____

List two items that went well today

_____

_____

List three things you are grateful for today

_____

_____

_____

Feel free to write any additional thoughts in this space

Today's Date: _____

List one challenge that you faced today

_____

List two items that went well today

_____

_____

List three things you are grateful for today

_____

_____

_____

Feel free to write any additional thoughts in this space

Today's Date: _____

List one challenge that you faced today

_____

List two items that went well today

_____

_____

List three things you are grateful for today

_____

_____

_____

Feel free to write any additional thoughts in this space

Today's Date: _____

List one challenge that you faced today

_____

List two items that went well today

_____

_____

List three things you are grateful for today

_____

_____

_____

Feel free to write any additional thoughts in this space

Today's Date: _____

List one challenge that you faced today
_____

List two items that went well today
_____

_____

List three things you are grateful for today
_____

_____

_____

Feel free to write any additional thoughts in this space

Today's Date: _____

List one challenge that you faced today

_____

List two items that went well today

_____

_____

List three things you are grateful for today

_____

_____

_____

Feel free to write any additional thoughts in this space

Today's Date: _____

List one challenge that you faced today
_____

List two items that went well today
_____

_____

List three things you are grateful for today
_____

_____

_____

Feel free to write any additional thoughts in this space

Today's Date: _____

List one challenge that you faced today

_____

List two items that went well today

_____

_____

List three things you are grateful for today

_____

_____

_____

Feel free to write any additional thoughts in this space

Today's Date: _____

List one challenge that you faced today
_____

List two items that went well today
_____
_____

List three things you are grateful for today
_____
_____
_____

Feel free to write any additional thoughts in this space

Today's Date: _____

List one challenge that you faced today

_____

List two items that went well today

_____

_____

List three things you are grateful for today

_____

_____

_____

Feel free to write any additional thoughts in this space

Today's Date: _____

Day 90 of your journey. When you took the time to write your ten-year plan, you wrote some goals that you were going to accomplish around the 90th day. How are you doing in them? Are you happy with your accomplishments or do you need to dedicate more time to your goals? Every month you get an extra page to update goals or do something artistic for yourself.

List one challenge that you faced today

_____

List two items that went well today

_____

_____

List three things you are grateful for today

_____

_____

_____

Feel free to write any additional thoughts in this space

Today's Date: _____

List one challenge that you faced today

_____

List two items that went well today

_____

_____

List three things you are grateful for today

_____

_____

_____

Feel free to write any additional thoughts in this space

Today's Date: _____

List one challenge that you faced today
_____

List two items that went well today
_____

_____

List three things you are grateful for today
_____

_____

_____

Feel free to write any additional thoughts in this space

Today's Date: _____

List one challenge that you faced today
_____

List two items that went well today
_____
_____

List three things you are grateful for today
_____
_____
_____

Feel free to write any additional thoughts in this space

Today's Date: _____

List one challenge that you faced today
_____

List two items that went well today
_____
_____

List three things you are grateful for today
_____
_____
_____

Feel free to write any additional thoughts in this space

Today's Date: _____

List one challenge that you faced today

_____

List two items that went well today

_____

_____

List three things you are grateful for today

_____

_____

_____

Feel free to write any additional thoughts in this space

Today's Date: _____

List one challenge that you faced today
_____

List two items that went well today
_____
_____

List three things you are grateful for today
_____
_____
_____

Feel free to write any additional thoughts in this space

Today's Date: _____

List one challenge that you faced today
_____

List two items that went well today
_____
_____

List three things you are grateful for today
_____
_____
_____

Feel free to write any additional thoughts in this space

Today's Date: _____

List one challenge that you faced today
_____

List two items that went well today
_____
_____

List three things you are grateful for today
_____
_____
_____

Feel free to write any additional thoughts in this space

Today's Date: _____

List one challenge that you faced today
_____

List two items that went well today
_____

_____

List three things you are grateful for today
_____

_____

_____

Feel free to write any additional thoughts in this space

Today's Date: _____

List one challenge that you faced today

_____

List two items that went well today

_____

_____

List three things you are grateful for today

_____

_____

_____

Feel free to write any additional thoughts in this space

Today's Date: _____

List one challenge that you faced today
_____

List two items that went well today
_____

_____

List three things you are grateful for today
_____

_____

_____

Feel free to write any additional thoughts in this space

Today's Date: _____

List one challenge that you faced today
_____

List two items that went well today
_____
_____

List three things you are grateful for today
_____
_____
_____

Feel free to write any additional thoughts in this space

Today's Date: _____

List one challenge that you faced today
_____

List two items that went well today
_____
_____

List three things you are grateful for today
_____
_____
_____

Feel free to write any additional thoughts in this space

Today's Date: _____

List one challenge that you faced today

_____

List two items that went well today

_____

_____

List three things you are grateful for today

_____

_____

_____

Feel free to write any additional thoughts in this space

Today's Date: _____

List one challenge that you faced today

_____

List two items that went well today

_____

_____

List three things you are grateful for today

_____

_____

_____

Feel free to write any additional thoughts in this space

Today's Date: _____

List one challenge that you faced today
_____

List two items that went well today
_____
_____

List three things you are grateful for today
_____
_____
_____

Feel free to write any additional thoughts in this space

Today's Date: _____

List one challenge that you faced today

_____

List two items that went well today

_____

_____

List three things you are grateful for today

_____

_____

_____

Feel free to write any additional thoughts in this space

Today's Date: _____

List one challenge that you faced today
_____

List two items that went well today
_____

_____

List three things you are grateful for today
_____

_____

_____

Feel free to write any additional thoughts in this space

Today's Date: _____

List one challenge that you faced today
_____

List two items that went well today
_____
_____

List three things you are grateful for today
_____
_____
_____

Feel free to write any additional thoughts in this space

Today's Date: _____

List one challenge that you faced today
_____

List two items that went well today
_____
_____

List three things you are grateful for today
_____
_____
_____

Feel free to write any additional thoughts in this space

Today's Date: _____

List one challenge that you faced today
_____

List two items that went well today
_____
_____

List three things you are grateful for today
_____
_____
_____

Feel free to write any additional thoughts in this space

Today's Date: _____

List one challenge that you faced today
_____

List two items that went well today
_____
_____

List three things you are grateful for today
_____
_____
_____

Feel free to write any additional thoughts in this space

Today's Date: _____

List one challenge that you faced today
_____

List two items that went well today
_____
_____

List three things you are grateful for today
_____
_____
_____

Feel free to write any additional thoughts in this space

Today's Date: _____

List one challenge that you faced today
_____

List two items that went well today
_____
_____

List three things you are grateful for today
_____
_____
_____

Feel free to write any additional thoughts in this space

Today's Date: _____

List one challenge that you faced today

_____

List two items that went well today

_____

_____

List three things you are grateful for today

_____

_____

_____

Feel free to write any additional thoughts in this space

Today's Date: _____

List one challenge that you faced today

_____

List two items that went well today

_____

_____

List three things you are grateful for today

_____

_____

_____

Feel free to write any additional thoughts in this space

Today's Date: _____

List one challenge that you faced today
_____

List two items that went well today
_____
_____

List three things you are grateful for today
_____
_____
_____

Feel free to write any additional thoughts in this space

Today's Date: _____

List one challenge that you faced today

_____

List two items that went well today

_____

_____

List three things you are grateful for today

_____

_____

_____

Feel free to write any additional thoughts in this space

Today's Date: _____

List one challenge that you faced today
_____

List two items that went well today
_____

_____

List three things you are grateful for today
_____

_____

_____

Feel free to write any additional thoughts in this space

Today's Date: _____

Welcome to day 120 of your journey. How has it been for you? Write about your challenges, frustrations and successes. Remember that nobody does it on their own; now, you should feel comfortable by now in raising your hand and asking for support. What agencies are around you that can support you in reaching your goals? There is plenty of space for you to write or draw.

List one challenge that you faced today

_____

List two items that went well today

_____

_____

List three things you are grateful for today

_____

_____

_____

Feel free to write any additional thoughts in this space

Today's Date: _____

List one challenge that you faced today
_____

List two items that went well today
_____

_____

List three things you are grateful for today
_____

_____

_____

Feel free to write any additional thoughts in this space

Today's Date: _____

List one challenge that you faced today
_____

List two items that went well today
_____

_____

List three things you are grateful for today
_____

_____

_____

Feel free to write any additional thoughts in this space

Today's Date: _____

List one challenge that you faced today

_____

List two items that went well today

_____

_____

List three things you are grateful for today

_____

_____

_____

Feel free to write any additional thoughts in this space

Today's Date: _____

List one challenge that you faced today

_____

List two items that went well today

_____

_____

List three things you are grateful for today

_____

_____

_____

Feel free to write any additional thoughts in this space

Today's Date: _____

List one challenge that you faced today

_____

List two items that went well today

_____

_____

List three things you are grateful for today

_____

_____

_____

Feel free to write any additional thoughts in this space

Today's Date: _____

List one challenge that you faced today
_____

List two items that went well today
_____
_____

List three things you are grateful for today
_____
_____
_____

Feel free to write any additional thoughts in this space

Today's Date: _____

List one challenge that you faced today
_____

List two items that went well today
_____
_____

List three things you are grateful for today
_____
_____
_____

Feel free to write any additional thoughts in this space

Today's Date: _____

List one challenge that you faced today
_____

List two items that went well today
_____
_____

List three things you are grateful for today
_____
_____
_____

Feel free to write any additional thoughts in this space

Today's Date: _____

List one challenge that you faced today

_____

List two items that went well today

_____

_____

List three things you are grateful for today

_____

_____

_____

Feel free to write any additional thoughts in this space

Today's Date: _____

List one challenge that you faced today
_____

List two items that went well today
_____

_____

List three things you are grateful for today
_____

_____

_____

Feel free to write any additional thoughts in this space

Today's Date: _____

List one challenge that you faced today

_____

List two items that went well today

_____

_____

List three things you are grateful for today

_____

_____

_____

Feel free to write any additional thoughts in this space

Today's Date: _____

List one challenge that you faced today
_____

List two items that went well today
_____
_____

List three things you are grateful for today
_____
_____
_____

Feel free to write any additional thoughts in this space

Today's Date: _____

List one challenge that you faced today

_____

List two items that went well today

_____

_____

List three things you are grateful for today

_____

_____

_____

Feel free to write any additional thoughts in this space

Today's Date: _____

List one challenge that you faced today
_____

List two items that went well today
_____

_____

List three things you are grateful for today
_____

_____

_____

Feel free to write any additional thoughts in this space

Today's Date: _____

List one challenge that you faced today

_____

List two items that went well today

_____

_____

List three things you are grateful for today

_____

_____

_____

Feel free to write any additional thoughts in this space

Today's Date: _____

List one challenge that you faced today
_____

List two items that went well today
_____
_____

List three things you are grateful for today
_____
_____
_____

Feel free to write any additional thoughts in this space

Today's Date: _____

List one challenge that you faced today

_____

List two items that went well today

_____

_____

List three things you are grateful for today

_____

_____

_____

Feel free to write any additional thoughts in this space

Today's Date: _____

List one challenge that you faced today
_____

List two items that went well today
_____
_____

List three things you are grateful for today
_____
_____
_____

Feel free to write any additional thoughts in this space

Today's Date: _____

List one challenge that you faced today

_____

List two items that went well today

_____

_____

List three things you are grateful for today

_____

_____

_____

Feel free to write any additional thoughts in this space

Today's Date: _____

List one challenge that you faced today
_____

List two items that went well today
_____
_____

List three things you are grateful for today
_____
_____
_____

Feel free to write any additional thoughts in this space

Today's Date: _____

List one challenge that you faced today

_____

List two items that went well today

_____

_____

List three things you are grateful for today

_____

_____

_____

Feel free to write any additional thoughts in this space

Today's Date: _____

List one challenge that you faced today

_____

List two items that went well today

_____

_____

List three things you are grateful for today

_____

_____

_____

Feel free to write any additional thoughts in this space

Today's Date: _____

List one challenge that you faced today

_____

List two items that went well today

_____

_____

List three things you are grateful for today

_____

_____

_____

Feel free to write any additional thoughts in this space

Today's Date: _____

List one challenge that you faced today
_____

List two items that went well today
_____
_____

List three things you are grateful for today
_____
_____
_____

Feel free to write any additional thoughts in this space

Today's Date: _____

List one challenge that you faced today

_____

List two items that went well today

_____

_____

List three things you are grateful for today

_____

_____

_____

Feel free to write any additional thoughts in this space

Today's Date: _____

List one challenge that you faced today
_____

List two items that went well today
_____

_____

List three things you are grateful for today
_____

_____

_____

Feel free to write any additional thoughts in this space

Today's Date: _____

List one challenge that you faced today
_____

List two items that went well today
_____

_____

List three things you are grateful for today
_____

_____

_____

Feel free to write any additional thoughts in this space

Today's Date: _____

List one challenge that you faced today
_____

List two items that went well today
_____
_____

List three things you are grateful for today
_____
_____
_____

Feel free to write any additional thoughts in this space

Today's Date: _____

List one challenge that you faced today

_____

List two items that went well today

_____

_____

List three things you are grateful for today

_____

_____

_____

Feel free to write any additional thoughts in this space

Today's Date: _____

It is day 150 of the journey. In life, there are many steps forward and a few setbacks. How many new friendships have you developed that are supportive of your success? How many individuals have you finally let go who were not supportive of your success? The journey is long, but worth it. Keep at it.

List one challenge that you faced today

_____

List two items that went well today

_____

_____

List three things you are grateful for today

_____

_____

_____

Feel free to write any additional thoughts in this space

Today's Date: _____

List one challenge that you faced today
_____

List two items that went well today
_____
_____

List three things you are grateful for today
_____
_____
_____

Feel free to write any additional thoughts in this space

Today's Date: _____

List one challenge that you faced today
_____

List two items that went well today
_____
_____

List three things you are grateful for today
_____
_____
_____

Feel free to write any additional thoughts in this space

Today's Date: _____

List one challenge that you faced today
_____

List two items that went well today
_____
_____

List three things you are grateful for today
_____
_____
_____

Feel free to write any additional thoughts in this space

Today's Date: _____

List one challenge that you faced today
_____

List two items that went well today
_____

_____

List three things you are grateful for today
_____

_____

_____

Feel free to write any additional thoughts in this space

Today's Date: _____

List one challenge that you faced today

_____

List two items that went well today

_____

_____

List three things you are grateful for today

_____

_____

_____

Feel free to write any additional thoughts in this space

Today's Date: _____

List one challenge that you faced today
_____

List two items that went well today
_____
_____

List three things you are grateful for today
_____
_____
_____

Feel free to write any additional thoughts in this space

Today's Date: _____

List one challenge that you faced today

_____

List two items that went well today

_____

_____

List three things you are grateful for today

_____

_____

_____

Feel free to write any additional thoughts in this space

Today's Date: _____

List one challenge that you faced today
_____

List two items that went well today
_____
_____

List three things you are grateful for today
_____
_____
_____

Feel free to write any additional thoughts in this space

Today's Date: _____

List one challenge that you faced today
_____

List two items that went well today
_____

_____

List three things you are grateful for today
_____

_____

_____

Feel free to write any additional thoughts in this space

Today's Date: _____

List one challenge that you faced today
_____

List two items that went well today
_____
_____

List three things you are grateful for today
_____
_____
_____

Feel free to write any additional thoughts in this space

Today's Date: _____

List one challenge that you faced today

_____

List two items that went well today

_____

_____

List three things you are grateful for today

_____

_____

_____

Feel free to write any additional thoughts in this space

Today's Date: _____

List one challenge that you faced today

_____

List two items that went well today

_____

_____

List three things you are grateful for today

_____

_____

_____

Feel free to write any additional thoughts in this space

Today's Date: _____

List one challenge that you faced today
_____

List two items that went well today
_____
_____

List three things you are grateful for today
_____
_____
_____

Feel free to write any additional thoughts in this space

Today's Date: _____

List one challenge that you faced today
_____

List two items that went well today
_____
_____

List three things you are grateful for today
_____
_____
_____

Feel free to write any additional thoughts in this space

Today's Date: _____

List one challenge that you faced today
_____

List two items that went well today
_____

_____

List three things you are grateful for today
_____

_____

_____

Feel free to write any additional thoughts in this space

Today's Date: _____

List one challenge that you faced today
_____

List two items that went well today
_____
_____

List three things you are grateful for today
_____
_____
_____

Feel free to write any additional thoughts in this space

Today's Date: _____

List one challenge that you faced today

_____

List two items that went well today

_____

_____

List three things you are grateful for today

_____

_____

_____

Feel free to write any additional thoughts in this space

Today's Date: _____

List one challenge that you faced today
_____

List two items that went well today
_____

_____

List three things you are grateful for today
_____

_____

_____

Feel free to write any additional thoughts in this space

Today's Date: _____

List one challenge that you faced today
_____

List two items that went well today
_____
_____

List three things you are grateful for today
_____
_____
_____

Feel free to write any additional thoughts in this space

Today's Date: _____

List one challenge that you faced today

_____

List two items that went well today

_____

_____

List three things you are grateful for today

_____

_____

_____

Feel free to write any additional thoughts in this space

Today's Date: _____

List one challenge that you faced today
_____

List two items that went well today
_____
_____

List three things you are grateful for today
_____
_____
_____

Feel free to write any additional thoughts in this space

Today's Date: _____

List one challenge that you faced today

_____

List two items that went well today

_____

_____

List three things you are grateful for today

_____

_____

_____

Feel free to write any additional thoughts in this space

Today's Date: _____

List one challenge that you faced today
_____

List two items that went well today
_____

_____

List three things you are grateful for today
_____

_____

_____

Feel free to write any additional thoughts in this space

Today's Date: _____

List one challenge that you faced today
_____

List two items that went well today
_____
_____

List three things you are grateful for today
_____
_____
_____

Feel free to write any additional thoughts in this space

Today's Date: _____

List one challenge that you faced today
_____

List two items that went well today
_____
_____

List three things you are grateful for today
_____
_____
_____

Feel free to write any additional thoughts in this space

Today's Date: _____

List one challenge that you faced today

_____

List two items that went well today

_____

_____

List three things you are grateful for today

_____

_____

_____

Feel free to write any additional thoughts in this space

Today's Date: _____

List one challenge that you faced today

_____

List two items that went well today

_____

_____

List three things you are grateful for today

_____

_____

_____

Feel free to write any additional thoughts in this space

Today's Date: _____

List one challenge that you faced today

_____

List two items that went well today

_____

_____

List three things you are grateful for today

_____

_____

_____

Feel free to write any additional thoughts in this space

Today's Date: _____

List one challenge that you faced today

_____

List two items that went well today

_____

_____

List three things you are grateful for today

_____

_____

_____

Feel free to write any additional thoughts in this space

Today's Date: _____

You have been working on your healing and success for 180 days or about 6 months. How do you feel? Are you comfortable with your progress? Have you abandoned enough negative influences and bad habits during this period of time? What new short goals have you decided to pursue that connect to your ten-year plan? You have two pages to do some writing and take some time to draw or add some art. This is the end of the first part of this journal. Part II is available for you to continue the work. I am proud of you for sticking with it. Keep going.

List one challenge that you faced today
_____

List two items that went well today
_____
_____

List three things you are grateful for today
_____
_____
_____

Feel free to write any additional thoughts in this space

MENTAL HEALTH RESOURCES		
National Suicide Prevention Hotline	(800) 273-8255	suicidepreventionlifeline.org
National Alliance on Mental Illness	(800) 950-6264	www.nami.org
UCLA Meditation Awareness		www.uclahealth.org/marc/mindful-meditations
Resource for Undocumented Immigrants		www.informedimmigrant.com/guides/daca-mental-health-providers/
LGBTQ RESOURCES		
The Trevor Project	(866) 488-7386	www.thetrevorproject.org
GOAL SETTING		
TED.com		www.ted.com/topics/goal-setting
$40,000 Scholarship		www.jkcf.org
Young People Empowered to Change The World		yparhub.berkeley.edu
CAREER PLANNING		
Jobs Made Real		www.jobsmadereal.com
Jobs of the Future		www.bls.gov/ooh/
Immigrants Rising		immigrantsrising.org
My Website		lideresdelfuturo.org
My Podcast	Lideres del Futuro	Spotify, Google Play, iTunes

CPSIA information can be obtained
at www.ICGtesting.com
Printed in the USA
BVHW041535240521
R12277600001B/R122776PG607713BVX00042B/26